Flower Blooms REVERSE Coloring Book

This book belongs to:

....

....

....

Inspiration

There are no rules! But you can try some of these ideas.

- flowers
- monsters
- faces
- tracing colors
- dotted lines
- dashed lines
- dots
- lines
- wiggly lines
- black lines
- white lines
- petals
- stacking shapes
- leave it
- rounded shapes
- circles
- shading
- double lines
- spirals
- leaves
- loops
- stacked lines
- squares
- bubbles
- stars
- hearts
- triangles
- color lines
- thick lines
- wobbly lines

You can use any tool you like. Experiment with different thicknesses, textures and colors. Find out which one you like the most. You'll be suprised by the effect.

Sample drawing

www.ingramcontent.com/pod-product-compliance
Lightning Source LLC
Chambersburg PA
CBHW062226220526
45471CB00009B/3358